YOUR DEDICATION AND

SINCERITY FOR GROWTH IS

SEEN AND APPRECIATED.

I'M EXCITED TO JOURNEY

WITH YOU IN THIS PROCESS.

WRITING THINGS DOWN IS EXTREMELY IMPORTANT IN THE CREATIVE PROCESS.

IT NOT ONLY CREATES ACCOUNTABILITY, BUT WRITING ALSO CREATES AND SENDS A VIBRATION TO THE UNIVERSE TO TRANSPIRE TO MAKE IT HAPPEN.

HOW YOU CAN USE THIS JOURNAL TO DEVOTE TIME FOR YOURSELF AND DEVELOP A DAILY PRACTICE FOR GROWTH:

1. DEDICATE A TIME OF THE DAY THAT WORKS BEST FOR YOUR SOLITUDE TO USE THIS JOURNAL.

2. FIND AN UNDISTURBED PLACE OR SPACE TO USE IT.

3. DETERMINE AND SET A FEASIBLE AMOUNT OF TIME TO DEDICATE TO THIS.

4. SET AND DETERMINE YOUR VIBE INTENTION FOR USING THIS JOURNAL.
   The next few pages will create the framework of the journal and help define your goals and your wellness

5. IMMERSE YOURSELF TO BE FULLY PRESENT THROUGH EACH SECTION,
   Feel and notice what arises without judgement

6. USE AND REPEAT DAILY.

[WATCH & LISTEN TO A GUIDED STEP-BY-STEP:]

CREATIVEVIBESONLY.COM/INTROJOURNAL

INTENTION(S)

"INTENTION IS THE CORE OF ALL CONSCIOUS LIFE. CONSCIOUS INTENTION COLORS AND MOVES EVERYTHING."

– HSING YUN

MERRIAM WEBSTER DEFINES INTENTION AS:
What one intends to do or bring about

WHAT DOES INTENTION MEAN TO YOU?
Spend a few minutes thinking about Intention(s) and what it means to you. As you think about it, write out and develop your own meaning and intention with this journal.

_____
_____
_____
_____
_____
_____
_____
_____
_____
_____

MERRIAM WEBSTER DEFINES WELLNESS AS:
The quality or state of being in good health especially as an actively sought goal.

WHAT DOES "WELLNESS" MEAN TO YOU?
Spend a few minutes thinking about wellness and what it means to you. As you think about it, write out and develop your own meaning.

_____
_____
_____
_____
_____
_____
_____
_____
_____
_____

GOALS

ARE EXTREMELY IMPORTANT IN THIS JOURNEY. IT'S THE BASELINE FOR YOUR GROWTH AND WHAT GROWTH COMES IN THIS PROCESS.

SET A GOAL.

CREATE.

REPEAT!

MERRIAM WEBSTER DEFINES A GOAL AS:
The terminal point of a race; the end toward which effort is directed.

SPEND A FEW MINUTES THINKING ABOUT HOW YOU DEFINE THE WORD "GOAL"
Additionally, think about and write your overall goal with your creativity and all the things you want to accomplish as an artist/creative. Where you want to go, who you want to work with, money you want to make, etc.

REVIEW YOUR LIST OF GOALS AND CATEGORIZE THIS LIST BASED ON PRIORITY OF: SHORT, MID, AND LONG-TERM.

SHORT:
(HAPPEN IMMEDIATELY – WITHIN 3 MONTHS)

....

....

....

....

....

MID:
(6-MONTHS - 2 YEARS)

....

....

....

....

....

LONG:
(2-5+ YEARS AND BEYOND)

....

....

....

....

....

MILESTONES

NOW SET SOME TIME-FRAMES/DATES THAT YOU CAN REALISTICALLY WORK BACK FROM TO KNOCK THESE GOALS OUT.

GOAL	TIME FRAME

IF THE TIME FRAME OR DATE IS 3 MONTHS AWAY, THINK ABOUT WHAT MILE-STONES YOU CAN PUT IN PLACE BETWEEN NOW AND THAT 3 MONTH DATE TO ACCOMPLISH THIS GOAL. WHAT FREQUENCY DOES THIS REQUIRE? A ONCE A DAY, ONCE A WEEK, ONCE EVERY TWO WEEKS OR ONCE A MONTH?

(NOT OVERWORKING OR SPREADING YOURSELF TOO THIN)

GOAL	TIME FRAME

"I AM" AFFIRMATIONS

ACCORDING TO MERRIAM WEBSTER

To "affirm" is to validate, confirm, assert as valid or state positively. When applied to your awareness, an affirmation is a statement of truth which one aspires to absorb into their life.

Affirmations are dynamic and practical — not wishful thinking. Affirmations can and do work because they are based on higher truths, we have yet to realize on a conscious level. According to Swami Kriyananda, "The greatest mistake people make is to belittle their own power to change themselves."
Self-improvement writer, Remez Sasson, says the repetition and corresponding mental images formed when saying affirmations help to change our subconscious mind.

The words "I am", which you consistently use to define who you are and what you are capable of, are the highest aspect of yourself.
Break lifelong habits of unwittingly besmirching this phrase. Discontinue using pejorative labels to cast aspersions on yourself. Always make your very first consideration the honoring of your Divinity. This will allow you to rise to previously unimagined heights.

In affirming "I AM" you teach your outer self to accept the unlimited power of your inner spirit and the things you place in your imagination can become true for you.

Write down and affirm who you are. Speak and repeat your affirmations in a quiet space with concentration. The repetition of your affirmation allows change to your habit patterns and attitudes over which we normally have little control. Train your subconscious mind daily with use of your affirmations throughout the day and even in challenging times.

IF NOT NOW, WHEN?

– HILLEL THE ELDER

"10 STEPS TO PROTECT YOUR VIBE"
–VEX KING

1. AVOID GOSSIP AND DRAMA
2. LET GO OF ANYTHING YOU CAN'T CONTROL.
3. AVOID COMPARING YOURSELF TO OTHERS
4. KEEP YOUR FAITH LARGER THAN YOUR FEARS
5. DON'T DO ANYTHING THAT DOESN'T FEEL RIGHT
6. DON'T BE AFRAID TO SPEND SOME TIME ALONE
7. SPEAK KINDLY TO YOURSELF AND OTHER PEOPLE
8. PLEASE YOURSELF BEFORE TRYING TO PLEASE OTHERS
9. STAY AWAY FROM PEOPLE WHO DRAIN YOUR ENERGY
10. IGNORE ANY OPINIONS THAT DON'T ENHANCE YOUR LIFE

MY DAILY VIBE

"Perseverance is a great element of success. If you knock long enough and loud enough at the gate, you are to wake up somebody."

- HENRY WADSWORTH LONGFELLOW

Date: _____

(MY) WELL-BEING CHECK IN:
How I'm feeling

....
....
....

(MY) GRATITUDE TODAY:
What, who and things I'm grateful for

....
....
....

(MY) INTENTION FOR TODAY:
What I hope/intend to accomplish or even create today?

....
....
....

(MY) GOAL FOR WHAT I'M WORKING ON AND CREATING:

....
....
....

I AM:
My affirmation for today

ADDITIONAL NOTES, THOUGHTS, REFLECTIONS, VIBES AND GRATITUDE:

What are you doing to get closer to your goals, intentions, and wellness? What are the challenges you are facing? What else comes up during your day to reflect on?

MY DAILY VIBE

"A positive state of mind leads to more meaningful actions."

Date: _____

❤️ (MY) WELL-BEING CHECK IN:
How I'm feeling

....
....
....

🙌 (MY) GRATITUDE TODAY:
What, who and things I'm grateful for

....
....
....

📅 (MY) INTENTION FOR TODAY:
What I hope/intend to accomplish or even create today?

....
....
....

🎯 (MY) GOAL FOR WHAT I'M WORKING ON AND CREATING:

....
....
....

💪 I AM:
My affirmation for today

ADDITIONAL NOTES, THOUGHTS, REFLECTIONS, VIBES AND GRATITUDE:

What are you doing to get closer to your goals, intentions, and wellness? What are the challenges you are facing? What else comes up during your day to reflect on?

MY DAILY VIBE

"It's impossible," said pride. "It's risky," said experience. "it's pointless," said reason. "Give it a try," whispered the heart."

Date: _____

(MY) WELL-BEING CHECK IN:
How I'm feeling

....
....
....

(MY) GRATITUDE TODAY:
What, who and things I'm grateful for

....
....
....

(MY) INTENTION FOR TODAY:
What I hope/intend to accomplish or even create today?

....
....
....

(MY) GOAL FOR WHAT I'M WORKING ON AND CREATING:

....
....
....

I AM:
My affirmation for today

ADDITIONAL NOTES, THOUGHTS, REFLECTIONS, VIBES AND GRATITUDE:

What are you doing to get closer to your goals, intentions, and wellness? What are the challenges you are facing? What else comes up during your day to reflect on?

MY DAILY VIBE

"A flower does not think of competing with the flower next to it. It just blooms."

- ZEN SHIN

Date: _____

(MY) WELL-BEING CHECK IN:
How I'm feeling

....
....
....

(MY) GRATITUDE TODAY:
What, who and things I'm grateful for

....
....
....

(MY) INTENTION FOR TODAY:
What I hope/intend to accomplish or even create today?

....
....
....

(MY) GOAL FOR WHAT I'M WORKING ON AND CREATING:

....
....
....

I AM:
My affirmation for today

ADDITIONAL NOTES, THOUGHTS, REFLECTIONS, VIBES AND GRATITUDE:

What are you doing to get closer to your goals, intentions, and wellness? What are the challenges you are facing? What else comes up during your day to reflect on?

MY DAILY VIBE

"A goal is a dream with a deadline."
- NAPOLEAN HILL

Date: _____

(MY) WELL-BEING CHECK IN:
How I'm feeling

....
....
....

(MY) GRATITUDE TODAY:
What, who and things I'm grateful for

....
....
....

(MY) INTENTION FOR TODAY:
What I hope/intend to accomplish or even create today?

....
....
....

(MY) GOAL FOR WHAT I'M WORKING ON AND CREATING:

....
....
....

I AM:
My affirmation for today

....

ADDITIONAL NOTES, THOUGHTS, REFLECTIONS, VIBES AND GRATITUDE:

What are you doing to get closer to your goals, intentions, and wellness? What are the challenges you are facing? What else comes up during your day to reflect on?

MY DAILY VIBE

"A mind is like a parachute. It doesn't work if it is not open."
- FRANK ZAPPA

Date: _____

(MY) WELL-BEING CHECK IN:
How I'm feeling

....
....
....

(MY) GRATITUDE TODAY:
What, who and things I'm grateful for

....
....
....

(MY) INTENTION FOR TODAY:
What I hope/intend to accomplish or even create today?

....
....
....

(MY) GOAL FOR WHAT I'M WORKING ON AND CREATING:

....
....
....

I AM:
My affirmation for today

ADDITIONAL NOTES, THOUGHTS, REFLECTIONS, VIBES AND GRATITUDE:

What are you doing to get closer to your goals, intentions, and wellness? What are the challenges you are facing? What else comes up during your day to reflect on?

MY DAILY VIBE

"Accept what God allows. There's always a reason."

Date: _____

❤️ (MY) WELL-BEING CHECK IN:
How I'm feeling

....
....
....

🙌 (MY) GRATITUDE TODAY:
What, who and things I'm grateful for

....
....
....

📅 (MY) INTENTION FOR TODAY:
What I hope/intend to accomplish or even create today?

....
....
....

🎯 (MY) GOAL FOR WHAT I'M WORKING ON AND CREATING:

....
....
....

💪 I AM:
My affirmation for today

....

ADDITIONAL NOTES, THOUGHTS, REFLECTIONS, VIBES AND GRATITUDE:

What are you doing to get closer to your goals, intentions, and wellness? What are the challenges you are facing? What else comes up during your day to reflect on?

MY DAILY VIBE

"All Happiness comes from awareness. The more we are conscious, the deeper the joy. Acceptance of pain, non-resistance, courage and endurance -- these open deep and perennial sources of real happiness, true bliss."

- NISARGADATTA MAHARAJ

Date: _____

(MY) WELL-BEING CHECK IN:
How I'm feeling

(MY) GRATITUDE TODAY:
What, who and things I'm grateful for

(MY) INTENTION FOR TODAY:
What I hope/intend to accomplish or even create today?

(MY) GOAL FOR WHAT I'M WORKING ON AND CREATING:

I AM:
My affirmation for today

ADDITIONAL NOTES, THOUGHTS, REFLECTIONS, VIBES AND GRATITUDE:

What are you doing to get closer to your goals, intentions, and wellness? What are the challenges you are facing? What else comes up during your day to reflect on?

MY DAILY VIBE

"All that we are is supremely divine. Trust the power of your energy, vibes and thoughts. Allow yourself to feel good about your greatness and your gifts. May you experience feelings of Good, abundance, joy, love, kindness and success."

- IAN DAVIS

Date: _____

(MY) WELL-BEING CHECK IN:
How I'm feeling

....
....
....

(MY) GRATITUDE TODAY:
What, who and things I'm grateful for

....
....
....

(MY) INTENTION FOR TODAY:
What I hope/intend to accomplish or even create today?

....
....
....

(MY) GOAL FOR WHAT I'M WORKING ON AND CREATING:

....
....
....

I AM:
My affirmation for today

ADDITIONAL NOTES, THOUGHTS, REFLECTIONS, VIBES AND GRATITUDE:

What are you doing to get closer to your goals, intentions, and wellness? What are the challenges you are facing? What else comes up during your day to reflect on?

MY DAILY VIBE

"All the things that truly matter, beauty, love creativity, joy and inner peace arise beyond the mind."

- EKHART TOLLE

Date: _____

(MY) WELL-BEING CHECK IN:
How I'm feeling

....
....
....

(MY) GRATITUDE TODAY:
What, who and things I'm grateful for

....
....
....

(MY) INTENTION FOR TODAY:
What I hope/intend to accomplish or even create today?

....
....
....

(MY) GOAL FOR WHAT I'M WORKING ON AND CREATING:

....
....
....

I AM:
My affirmation for today

ADDITIONAL NOTES, THOUGHTS, REFLECTIONS, VIBES AND GRATITUDE:

What are you doing to get closer to your goals, intentions, and wellness? What are the challenges you are facing? What else comes up during your day to reflect on?

MY DAILY VIBE

"Allow your passion to become your purpose, and it will one day become your profession."

- GABRIELLE BERNSTEIN

Date: _____

(MY) WELL-BEING CHECK IN:
How I'm feeling

....
....
....

(MY) GRATITUDE TODAY:
What, who and things I'm grateful for

....
....
....

(MY) INTENTION FOR TODAY:
What I hope/intend to accomplish or even create today?

....
....
....

(MY) GOAL FOR WHAT I'M WORKING ON AND CREATING:

....
....
....

I AM:
My affirmation for today

....

ADDITIONAL NOTES, THOUGHTS, REFLECTIONS, VIBES AND GRATITUDE:

What are you doing to get closer to your goals, intentions, and wellness? What are the challenges you are facing? What else comes up during your day to reflect on?

MY DAILY VIBE

"Perseverance is a great element of success. If you knock long enough and loud enough at the gate, you are to wake up somebody."

- HENRY WADSWORTH LONGFELLOW

Date: _____

(MY) WELL-BEING CHECK IN:
How I'm feeling

....
....
....

(MY) GRATITUDE TODAY:
What, who and things I'm grateful for

....
....
....

(MY) INTENTION FOR TODAY:
What I hope/intend to accomplish or even create today?

....
....
....

(MY) GOAL FOR WHAT I'M WORKING ON AND CREATING:

....
....
....

I AM:
My affirmation for today

ADDITIONAL NOTES, THOUGHTS, REFLECTIONS, VIBES AND GRATITUDE:

What are you doing to get closer to your goals, intentions, and wellness? What are the challenges you are facing? What else comes up during your day to reflect on?

MY DAILY VIBE

"Allow yourself to be happy. Protect your space. Create boundaries. Decide what holds your attention. Spend time the way you choose. Give consent to yourself. It starts within. Inhale, and give yourself gratitude. Exhale and release, a smile."

- IAN DAVIS

Date: _____

(MY) WELL-BEING CHECK IN:
How I'm feeling

....
....
....

(MY) GRATITUDE TODAY:
What, who and things I'm grateful for

....
....
....

(MY) INTENTION FOR TODAY:
What I hope/intend to accomplish or even create today?

....
....
....

(MY) GOAL FOR WHAT I'M WORKING ON AND CREATING:

....
....
....

I AM:
My affirmation for today

ADDITIONAL NOTES, THOUGHTS, REFLECTIONS, VIBES AND GRATITUDE:

What are you doing to get closer to your goals, intentions, and wellness? What are the challenges you are facing? What else comes up during your day to reflect on?

MY DAILY VIBE

"Always leave people better than you found them. Hug the hurt. Kiss the broken. Befriend the lost. Love the lonely."

- MW

Date: _____

(MY) WELL-BEING CHECK IN:
How I'm feeling

....
....
....

(MY) GRATITUDE TODAY:
What, who and things I'm grateful for

....
....
....

(MY) INTENTION FOR TODAY:
What I hope/intend to accomplish or even create today?

....
....
....

(MY) GOAL FOR WHAT I'M WORKING ON AND CREATING:

....
....
....

I AM:
My affirmation for today

ADDITIONAL NOTES, THOUGHTS, REFLECTIONS, VIBES AND GRATITUDE:

What are you doing to get closer to your goals, intentions, and wellness? What are the challenges you are facing? What else comes up during your day to reflect on?

MY DAILY VIBE

"As i look back on my life, i realize that every time i thought i was being rejected from something good, i was actually being re-directed to something better."

- STEVE MARABOLI

Date: _____

(MY) WELL-BEING CHECK IN:
How I'm feeling

....
....
....

(MY) GRATITUDE TODAY:
What, who and things I'm grateful for

....
....
....

(MY) INTENTION FOR TODAY:
What I hope/intend to accomplish or even create today?

....
....
....

(MY) GOAL FOR WHAT I'M WORKING ON AND CREATING:

....
....
....

I AM:
My affirmation for today

ADDITIONAL NOTES, THOUGHTS, REFLECTIONS, VIBES AND GRATITUDE:

What are you doing to get closer to your goals, intentions, and wellness? What are the challenges you are facing? What else comes up during your day to reflect on?

MY DAILY VIBE

"As my sufferings mounted i soone realized that there were two ways in which I could respond... either to react with bitterness or seek to transform the suffering into a creative force."

- DR. MARTIN LUTHER KING JR.

Date: _____

(MY) WELL-BEING CHECK IN:
How I'm feeling

....
....
....

(MY) GRATITUDE TODAY:
What, who and things I'm grateful for

....
....
....

(MY) INTENTION FOR TODAY:
What I hope/intend to accomplish or even create today?

....
....
....

(MY) GOAL FOR WHAT I'M WORKING ON AND CREATING:

....
....
....

I AM:
My affirmation for today

....

ADDITIONAL NOTES, THOUGHTS, REFLECTIONS, VIBES AND GRATITUDE:

What are you doing to get closer to your goals, intentions, and wellness? What are the challenges you are facing? What else comes up during your day to reflect on?

MY DAILY VIBE

"As we arise each morning let us determine to respond with more love and kindness to whatever might come our way."

- THOMAS S. MONSON

Date: _____

(MY) WELL-BEING CHECK IN:
How I'm feeling

....
....
....

(MY) GRATITUDE TODAY:
What, who and things I'm grateful for

....
....
....

(MY) INTENTION FOR TODAY:
What I hope/intend to accomplish or even create today?

....
....
....

(MY) GOAL FOR WHAT I'M WORKING ON AND CREATING:

....
....
....

I AM:
My affirmation for today

ADDITIONAL NOTES, THOUGHTS, REFLECTIONS, VIBES AND GRATITUDE:

What are you doing to get closer to your goals, intentions, and wellness? What are the challenges you are facing? What else comes up during your day to reflect on?

MY DAILY VIBE

"As you think, so you shall become."
- BRUCE LEE

Date: _____

(MY) WELL-BEING CHECK IN:
How I'm feeling

....
....
....

(MY) GRATITUDE TODAY:
What, who and things I'm grateful for

....
....
....

(MY) INTENTION FOR TODAY:
What I hope/intend to accomplish or even create today?

....
....
....

(MY) GOAL FOR WHAT I'M WORKING ON AND CREATING:

....
....
....

I AM:
My affirmation for today

ADDITIONAL NOTES, THOUGHTS, REFLECTIONS, VIBES AND GRATITUDE:

What are you doing to get closer to your goals, intentions, and wellness? What are the challenges you are facing? What else comes up during your day to reflect on?

MY DAILY VIBE

"As you vibrate higher you attract more genuine people who vibrate higher too."

- LALAH DELIA

Date: _____

(MY) WELL-BEING CHECK IN:
How I'm feeling

....
....
....

(MY) GRATITUDE TODAY:
What, who and things I'm grateful for

....
....
....

(MY) INTENTION FOR TODAY:
What I hope/intend to accomplish or even create today?

....
....
....

(MY) GOAL FOR WHAT I'M WORKING ON AND CREATING:

....
....
....

I AM:
My affirmation for today

ADDITIONAL NOTES, THOUGHTS, REFLECTIONS, VIBES AND GRATITUDE:

What are you doing to get closer to your goals, intentions, and wellness? What are the challenges you are facing? What else comes up during your day to reflect on?

MY DAILY VIBE

"At the end of life, what really attrs is not what we bought but what we built; not what we got but what we shared; not our competence but our character; and not our success, but our significance. Live a life that matters. Live a life of love."

Date: _____

(MY) WELL-BEING CHECK IN:
How I'm feeling

....
....
....

(MY) GRATITUDE TODAY:
What, who and things I'm grateful for

....
....
....

(MY) INTENTION FOR TODAY:
What I hope/intend to accomplish or even create today?

....
....
....

(MY) GOAL FOR WHAT I'M WORKING ON AND CREATING:

....
....
....

I AM:
My affirmation for today

ADDITIONAL NOTES, THOUGHTS, REFLECTIONS, VIBES AND GRATITUDE:

What are you doing to get closer to your goals, intentions, and wellness? What are the challenges you are facing? What else comes up during your day to reflect on?

MY DAILY VIBE

"Average people have wishes and hopes. Confident people have goals and plans."

- BRIAN TRACY

Date: _____

(MY) WELL-BEING CHECK IN:
How I'm feeling

....
....
....

(MY) GRATITUDE TODAY:
What, who and things I'm grateful for

....
....
....

(MY) INTENTION FOR TODAY:
What I hope/intend to accomplish or even create today?

....
....
....

(MY) GOAL FOR WHAT I'M WORKING ON AND CREATING:

....
....
....

I AM:
My affirmation for today

ADDITIONAL NOTES, THOUGHTS, REFLECTIONS, VIBES AND GRATITUDE:

What are you doing to get closer to your goals, intentions, and wellness? What are the challenges you are facing? What else comes up during your day to reflect on?

MY DAILY VIBE

"Be a warrior, not a worrier."

Date: _____

(MY) WELL-BEING CHECK IN:
How I'm feeling

....
....
....

(MY) GRATITUDE TODAY:
What, who and things I'm grateful for

....
....
....

(MY) INTENTION FOR TODAY:
What I hope/intend to accomplish or even create today?

....
....
....

(MY) GOAL FOR WHAT I'M WORKING ON AND CREATING:

....
....
....

I AM:
My affirmation for today

ADDITIONAL NOTES, THOUGHTS, REFLECTIONS, VIBES AND GRATITUDE:

What are you doing to get closer to your goals, intentions, and wellness? What are the challenges you are facing? What else comes up during your day to reflect on?

MY DAILY VIBE

"Be Awesome today."

Date: _____

❤️ (MY) WELL-BEING CHECK IN:
How I'm feeling

....
....
....

🙌 (MY) GRATITUDE TODAY:
What, who and things I'm grateful for

....
....
....

📅 (MY) INTENTION FOR TODAY:
What I hope/intend to accomplish or even create today?

....
....
....

🎯 (MY) GOAL FOR WHAT I'M WORKING ON AND CREATING:

....
....
....

💪 I AM:
My affirmation for today

....

ADDITIONAL NOTES, THOUGHTS, REFLECTIONS, VIBES AND GRATITUDE:

What are you doing to get closer to your goals, intentions, and wellness? What are the challenges you are facing? What else comes up during your day to reflect on?

MY DAILY VIBE

"Be brave. Even if you're not, pretend to be."
- H. JACKSON BROWN JR.

Date: _____

(MY) WELL-BEING CHECK IN:
How I'm feeling

....
....
....

(MY) GRATITUDE TODAY:
What, who and things I'm grateful for

....
....
....

(MY) INTENTION FOR TODAY:
What I hope/intend to accomplish or even create today?

....
....
....

(MY) GOAL FOR WHAT I'M WORKING ON AND CREATING:

....
....
....

I AM:
My affirmation for today

ADDITIONAL NOTES, THOUGHTS, REFLECTIONS, VIBES AND GRATITUDE:

What are you doing to get closer to your goals, intentions, and wellness? What are the challenges you are facing? What else comes up during your day to reflect on?

MY DAILY VIBE

"Be content with what you have; rejoice in the way things are. When you realize there is nothing lacking, the whole world belongs to you."

- LAO TZU

Date: _____

(MY) WELL-BEING CHECK IN:
How I'm feeling

....
....
....

(MY) GRATITUDE TODAY:
What, who and things I'm grateful for

....
....
....

(MY) INTENTION FOR TODAY:
What I hope/intend to accomplish or even create today?

....
....
....

(MY) GOAL FOR WHAT I'M WORKING ON AND CREATING:

....
....
....

I AM:
My affirmation for today

ADDITIONAL NOTES, THOUGHTS, REFLECTIONS, VIBES AND GRATITUDE:

What are you doing to get closer to your goals, intentions, and wellness? What are the challenges you are facing? What else comes up during your day to reflect on?

MY DAILY VIBE

"Be daring, be different, be impractical; be anything that will assert integrity of purpose and imaginative vision against the play-it-safers, the creatures of the commonplace, the slaves of the ordinary."

- CECIL BEATON

Date: _____

(MY) WELL-BEING CHECK IN:
How I'm feeling

(MY) GRATITUDE TODAY:
What, who and things I'm grateful for

(MY) INTENTION FOR TODAY:
What I hope/intend to accomplish or even create today?

(MY) GOAL FOR WHAT I'M WORKING ON AND CREATING:

I AM:
My affirmation for today

ADDITIONAL NOTES, THOUGHTS, REFLECTIONS, VIBES AND GRATITUDE:

What are you doing to get closer to your goals, intentions, and wellness? What are the challenges you are facing? What else comes up during your day to reflect on?

MY DAILY VIBE

"Be happy with the little you have. There are some people with nothing who still manage to smile."

Date: _____

(MY) WELL-BEING CHECK IN:
How I'm feeling

....
....
....

(MY) GRATITUDE TODAY:
What, who and things I'm grateful for

....
....
....

(MY) INTENTION FOR TODAY:
What I hope/intend to accomplish or even create today?

....
....
....

(MY) GOAL FOR WHAT I'M WORKING ON AND CREATING:

....
....
....

I AM:
My affirmation for today

ADDITIONAL NOTES, THOUGHTS, REFLECTIONS, VIBES AND GRATITUDE:

What are you doing to get closer to your goals, intentions, and wellness? What are the challenges you are facing? What else comes up during your day to reflect on?

MY DAILY VIBE

"Be here now."

Date: _____

❤️ (MY) WELL-BEING CHECK IN:
How I'm feeling

....
....
....

🙌 (MY) GRATITUDE TODAY:
What, who and things I'm grateful for

....
....
....

📅 (MY) INTENTION FOR TODAY:
What I hope/intend to accomplish or even create today?

....
....
....

🎯 (MY) GOAL FOR WHAT I'M WORKING ON AND CREATING:

....
....
....

💪 I AM:
My affirmation for today

....

ADDITIONAL NOTES, THOUGHTS, REFLECTIONS, VIBES AND GRATITUDE:

What are you doing to get closer to your goals, intentions, and wellness? What are the challenges you are facing? What else comes up during your day to reflect on?

MY DAILY VIBE

"Be open to a work's strengths and weaknesses. As opposed to solely focusing on a weakness, allowing it to overwhelm the strengths."

- RICK RUBIN

Date: _____

(MY) WELL-BEING CHECK IN:
How I'm feeling

....
....
....

(MY) GRATITUDE TODAY:
What, who and things I'm grateful for

....
....
....

(MY) INTENTION FOR TODAY:
What I hope/intend to accomplish or even create today?

....
....
....

(MY) GOAL FOR WHAT I'M WORKING ON AND CREATING:

....
....
....

I AM:
My affirmation for today

....

ADDITIONAL NOTES, THOUGHTS, REFLECTIONS, VIBES AND GRATITUDE:

What are you doing to get closer to your goals, intentions, and wellness? What are the challenges you are facing? What else comes up during your day to reflect on?

MY DAILY VIBE

"Be patient. Good things will come to those who wait and continue to work hard."

Date: _____

(MY) WELL-BEING CHECK IN:
How I'm feeling

....
....
....

(MY) GRATITUDE TODAY:
What, who and things I'm grateful for

....
....
....

(MY) INTENTION FOR TODAY:
What I hope/intend to accomplish or even create today?

....
....
....

(MY) GOAL FOR WHAT I'M WORKING ON AND CREATING:

....
....
....

I AM:
My affirmation for today

ADDITIONAL NOTES, THOUGHTS, REFLECTIONS, VIBES AND GRATITUDE:

What are you doing to get closer to your goals, intentions, and wellness? What are the challenges you are facing? What else comes up during your day to reflect on?

A FLOWER DOES NOT THINK OF COMPETING WITH THE FLOWER NEXT TO IT.
IT JUST BLOOMS

– ZEN SHIN

MY TARGETS FOR THE MONTH OF: _____

NOTES

MY DAILY VIBE

"Be so good they can't ignore you."
- STEVE MARTIN

Date: _____

♥ (MY) WELL-BEING CHECK IN:
How I'm feeling

....
....
....

🙌 (MY) GRATITUDE TODAY:
What, who and things I'm grateful for

....
....
....

📅 (MY) INTENTION FOR TODAY:
What I hope/intend to accomplish or even create today?

....
....
....

🎯 (MY) GOAL FOR WHAT I'M WORKING ON AND CREATING:

....
....
....

💪 I AM:
My affirmation for today

....

ADDITIONAL NOTES, THOUGHTS, REFLECTIONS, VIBES AND GRATITUDE:

What are you doing to get closer to your goals, intentions, and wellness? What are the challenges you are facing? What else comes up during your day to reflect on?

MY DAILY VIBE

"Be strong, you never know who you are inspiring."

Date: _____

(MY) WELL-BEING CHECK IN:
How I'm feeling

....
....
....

(MY) GRATITUDE TODAY:
What, who and things I'm grateful for

....
....
....

(MY) INTENTION FOR TODAY:
What I hope/intend to accomplish or even create today?

....
....
....

(MY) GOAL FOR WHAT I'M WORKING ON AND CREATING:

....
....
....

I AM:
My affirmation for today

....

ADDITIONAL NOTES, THOUGHTS, REFLECTIONS, VIBES AND GRATITUDE:

What are you doing to get closer to your goals, intentions, and wellness? What are the challenges you are facing? What else comes up during your day to reflect on?

MY DAILY VIBE

"Being cool is being your won self, not doing something that someone else is telling you to do."

- VANESSA HUDGENS

Date: _____

(MY) WELL-BEING CHECK IN:
How I'm feeling

....
....
....

(MY) GRATITUDE TODAY:
What, who and things I'm grateful for

....
....
....

(MY) INTENTION FOR TODAY:
What I hope/intend to accomplish or even create today?

....
....
....

(MY) GOAL FOR WHAT I'M WORKING ON AND CREATING:

....
....
....

I AM:
My affirmation for today

ADDITIONAL NOTES, THOUGHTS, REFLECTIONS, VIBES AND GRATITUDE:

What are you doing to get closer to your goals, intentions, and wellness? What are the challenges you are facing? What else comes up during your day to reflect on?

MY DAILY VIBE

"Being defeated is often a temporary condition. Giving up is what makes it permanent."

- MARILYN VOS SAVANT

Date: _____

(MY) WELL-BEING CHECK IN:
How I'm feeling

....
....
....

(MY) GRATITUDE TODAY:
What, who and things I'm grateful for

....
....
....

(MY) INTENTION FOR TODAY:
What I hope/intend to accomplish or even create today?

....
....
....

(MY) GOAL FOR WHAT I'M WORKING ON AND CREATING:

....
....
....

I AM:
My affirmation for today

ADDITIONAL NOTES, THOUGHTS, REFLECTIONS, VIBES AND GRATITUDE:

What are you doing to get closer to your goals, intentions, and wellness? What are the challenges you are facing? What else comes up during your day to reflect on?

MY DAILY VIBE

"Belief in oneself is increadibly infectious. It generates momentum, the collective force of which far outweighs any kernel of self-doubt that may creep in."

- AIMEE MULLINS

Date: _____

(MY) WELL-BEING CHECK IN:
How I'm feeling

(MY) GRATITUDE TODAY:
What, who and things I'm grateful for

(MY) INTENTION FOR TODAY:
What I hope/intend to accomplish or even create today?

(MY) GOAL FOR WHAT I'M WORKING ON AND CREATING:

I AM:
My affirmation for today

ADDITIONAL NOTES, THOUGHTS, REFLECTIONS, VIBES AND GRATITUDE:

What are you doing to get closer to your goals, intentions, and wellness? What are the challenges you are facing? What else comes up during your day to reflect on?

MY DAILY VIBE

*"Believe in yourself.
The greatest success is being yourself."*

Date: _____

(MY) WELL-BEING CHECK IN:
How I'm feeling

....
....
....

(MY) GRATITUDE TODAY:
What, who and things I'm grateful for

....
....
....

(MY) INTENTION FOR TODAY:
What I hope/intend to accomplish or even create today?

....
....
....

(MY) GOAL FOR WHAT I'M WORKING ON AND CREATING:

....
....
....

I AM:
My affirmation for today

ADDITIONAL NOTES, THOUGHTS, REFLECTIONS, VIBES AND GRATITUDE:

What are you doing to get closer to your goals, intentions, and wellness? What are the challenges you are facing? What else comes up during your day to reflect on?

MY DAILY VIBE

"Believe me, the reward is not so great without the struggle."
- WILMA RUDOLPH

Date: _____

(MY) WELL-BEING CHECK IN:
How I'm feeling

....
....
....

(MY) GRATITUDE TODAY:
What, who and things I'm grateful for

....
....
....

(MY) INTENTION FOR TODAY:
What I hope/intend to accomplish or even create today?

....
....
....

(MY) GOAL FOR WHAT I'M WORKING ON AND CREATING:

....
....
....

I AM:
My affirmation for today

ADDITIONAL NOTES, THOUGHTS, REFLECTIONS, VIBES AND GRATITUDE:

What are you doing to get closer to your goals, intentions, and wellness? What are the challenges you are facing? What else comes up during your day to reflect on?

MY DAILY VIBE

"Believe with all of your heart that you will do what you were made to."
- ORISON SWETT MARDEN

Date: _____

(MY) WELL-BEING CHECK IN:
How I'm feeling

....
....
....

(MY) GRATITUDE TODAY:
What, who and things I'm grateful for

....
....
....

(MY) INTENTION FOR TODAY:
What I hope/intend to accomplish or even create today?

....
....
....

(MY) GOAL FOR WHAT I'M WORKING ON AND CREATING:

....
....
....

I AM:
My affirmation for today

....

ADDITIONAL NOTES, THOUGHTS, REFLECTIONS, VIBES AND GRATITUDE:

What are you doing to get closer to your goals, intentions, and wellness? What are the challenges you are facing? What else comes up during your day to reflect on?

MY DAILY VIBE

"Believing that you can move mountains sometimes is more important than having the ability to do so."

\- JOSHUA KUSHNER

Date: _____

(MY) WELL-BEING CHECK IN:
How I'm feeling

....
....
....

(MY) GRATITUDE TODAY:
What, who and things I'm grateful for

....
....
....

(MY) INTENTION FOR TODAY:
What I hope/intend to accomplish or even create today?

....
....
....

(MY) GOAL FOR WHAT I'M WORKING ON AND CREATING:

....
....
....

I AM:
My affirmation for today

....

ADDITIONAL NOTES, THOUGHTS, REFLECTIONS, VIBES AND GRATITUDE:

What are you doing to get closer to your goals, intentions, and wellness? What are the challenges you are facing? What else comes up during your day to reflect on?

MY DAILY VIBE

"Big shots are only little shots who keep shooting."
- CHRISTOPHER MORELY

Date: _____

(MY) WELL-BEING CHECK IN:
How I'm feeling

....
....
....

(MY) GRATITUDE TODAY:
What, who and things I'm grateful for

....
....
....

(MY) INTENTION FOR TODAY:
What I hope/intend to accomplish or even create today?

....
....
....

(MY) GOAL FOR WHAT I'M WORKING ON AND CREATING:

....
....
....

I AM:
My affirmation for today

ADDITIONAL NOTES, THOUGHTS, REFLECTIONS, VIBES AND GRATITUDE:

What are you doing to get closer to your goals, intentions, and wellness? What are the challenges you are facing? What else comes up during your day to reflect on?

MY DAILY VIBE

"Breath is the bridge which connects life to consciousness, which unites your body to your thoughts. Whenever your mind becomes scattered, use your breath as the means to take hold of your mind again."

- THICH NHAT HANH

Date: _____

(MY) WELL-BEING CHECK IN:
How I'm feeling

....
....
....

(MY) GRATITUDE TODAY:
What, who and things I'm grateful for

....
....
....

(MY) INTENTION FOR TODAY:
What I hope/intend to accomplish or even create today?

....
....
....

(MY) GOAL FOR WHAT I'M WORKING ON AND CREATING:

....
....
....

I AM:
My affirmation for today

ADDITIONAL NOTES, THOUGHTS, REFLECTIONS, VIBES AND GRATITUDE:

What are you doing to get closer to your goals, intentions, and wellness? What are the challenges you are facing? What else comes up during your day to reflect on?

MY DAILY VIBE

"Breathe. Bring your mind back to this current moment. Any other moment, whether past or future is not occurring. Right now is what's happening. Right now is what's to be experienced."

— NICOLE ADDISON

Date: _____

(MY) WELL-BEING CHECK IN:
How I'm feeling

....
....
....

(MY) GRATITUDE TODAY:
What, who and things I'm grateful for

....
....
....

(MY) INTENTION FOR TODAY:
What I hope/intend to accomplish or even create today?

....
....
....

(MY) GOAL FOR WHAT I'M WORKING ON AND CREATING:

....
....
....

I AM:
My affirmation for today

ADDITIONAL NOTES, THOUGHTS, REFLECTIONS, VIBES AND GRATITUDE:

What are you doing to get closer to your goals, intentions, and wellness? What are the challenges you are facing? What else comes up during your day to reflect on?

MY DAILY VIBE

"But we also believe in taking risks, because that's how you move things along."

- MELINDA GATES

Date: _____

(MY) WELL-BEING CHECK IN:
How I'm feeling

....
....
....

(MY) GRATITUDE TODAY:
What, who and things I'm grateful for

....
....
....

(MY) INTENTION FOR TODAY:
What I hope/intend to accomplish or even create today?

....
....
....

(MY) GOAL FOR WHAT I'M WORKING ON AND CREATING:

....
....
....

I AM:
My affirmation for today

ADDITIONAL NOTES, THOUGHTS, REFLECTIONS, VIBES AND GRATITUDE:

What are you doing to get closer to your goals, intentions, and wellness? What are the challenges you are facing? What else comes up during your day to reflect on?

MY DAILY VIBE

> *"Caring about what people think of you is useless. Most people don't even know what they think of themselves."*
>
> - SONYA TECLAI

Date: _____

❤️ (MY) WELL-BEING CHECK IN:
How I'm feeling

....
....
....

🙌 (MY) GRATITUDE TODAY:
What, who and things I'm grateful for

....
....
....

📅 (MY) INTENTION FOR TODAY:
What I hope/intend to accomplish or even create today?

....
....
....

🎯 (MY) GOAL FOR WHAT I'M WORKING ON AND CREATING:

....
....
....

💪 I AM:
My affirmation for today

ADDITIONAL NOTES, THOUGHTS, REFLECTIONS, VIBES AND GRATITUDE:

What are you doing to get closer to your goals, intentions, and wellness? What are the challenges you are facing? What else comes up during your day to reflect on?

MY DAILY VIBE

"Challenges are what make life interesting. Overcoming them is what makes them meaningful."

- JOSHUA J. MARINE

Date: _____

(MY) WELL-BEING CHECK IN:
How I'm feeling

....
....
....

(MY) GRATITUDE TODAY:
What, who and things I'm grateful for

....
....
....

(MY) INTENTION FOR TODAY:
What I hope/intend to accomplish or even create today?

....
....
....

(MY) GOAL FOR WHAT I'M WORKING ON AND CREATING:

....
....
....

I AM:
My affirmation for today

ADDITIONAL NOTES, THOUGHTS, REFLECTIONS, VIBES AND GRATITUDE:

What are you doing to get closer to your goals, intentions, and wellness? What are the challenges you are facing? What else comes up during your day to reflect on?

MY DAILY VIBE

"Change your thoughts and you change your world."
- NORMAN VINCENT PEALE

Date: _____

(MY) WELL-BEING CHECK IN:
How I'm feeling

....
....
....

(MY) GRATITUDE TODAY:
What, who and things I'm grateful for

....
....
....

(MY) INTENTION FOR TODAY:
What I hope/intend to accomplish or even create today?

....
....
....

(MY) GOAL FOR WHAT I'M WORKING ON AND CREATING:

....
....
....

I AM:
My affirmation for today

ADDITIONAL NOTES, THOUGHTS, REFLECTIONS, VIBES AND GRATITUDE:

What are you doing to get closer to your goals, intentions, and wellness? What are the challenges you are facing? What else comes up during your day to reflect on?

MY DAILY VIBE

"Choosing to be positive and having a grateful attitude is going to determine how you're going to live your life."

- JOEL OSTEEN

Date: _____

(MY) WELL-BEING CHECK IN:
How I'm feeling

....
....
....

(MY) GRATITUDE TODAY:
What, who and things I'm grateful for

....
....
....

(MY) INTENTION FOR TODAY:
What I hope/intend to accomplish or even create today?

....
....
....

(MY) GOAL FOR WHAT I'M WORKING ON AND CREATING:

....
....
....

I AM:
My affirmation for today

ADDITIONAL NOTES, THOUGHTS, REFLECTIONS, VIBES AND GRATITUDE:

What are you doing to get closer to your goals, intentions, and wellness? What are the challenges you are facing? What else comes up during your day to reflect on?

MY DAILY VIBE

"Claim your power to feel good. Feeling good is feeling god. When we feel good, we remember and recognize the god within us. May you Recognize and use the power of the words "I am". May you feel, good, abundance and fulfillment. Deep inhale, smile, exhale and release."

– IAN DAVIS

Date: _____

(MY) WELL-BEING CHECK IN:
How I'm feeling

....
....
....

(MY) GRATITUDE TODAY:
What, who and things I'm grateful for

....
....
....

(MY) INTENTION FOR TODAY:
What I hope/intend to accomplish or even create today?

....
....
....

(MY) GOAL FOR WHAT I'M WORKING ON AND CREATING:

....
....
....

I AM:
My affirmation for today

ADDITIONAL NOTES, THOUGHTS, REFLECTIONS, VIBES AND GRATITUDE:

What are you doing to get closer to your goals, intentions, and wellness? What are the challenges you are facing? What else comes up during your day to reflect on?

MY DAILY VIBE

"Clear your mind of can't."
- SAMUEL JOHNSON

Date: _____

(MY) WELL-BEING CHECK IN:
How I'm feeling

....
....
....

(MY) GRATITUDE TODAY:
What, who and things I'm grateful for

....
....
....

(MY) INTENTION FOR TODAY:
What I hope/intend to accomplish or even create today?

....
....
....

(MY) GOAL FOR WHAT I'M WORKING ON AND CREATING:

....
....
....

I AM:
My affirmation for today

....

ADDITIONAL NOTES, THOUGHTS, REFLECTIONS, VIBES AND GRATITUDE:

What are you doing to get closer to your goals, intentions, and wellness? What are the challenges you are facing? What else comes up during your day to reflect on?

MY DAILY VIBE

> *"Coming together is a beginning; keeping together is progress; working together is success."*
>
> – HENRY FORD

Date: _____

(MY) WELL-BEING CHECK IN:
How I'm feeling

_____
_____
_____

(MY) GRATITUDE TODAY:
What, who and things I'm grateful for

_____
_____
_____

(MY) INTENTION FOR TODAY:
What I hope/intend to accomplish or even create today?

_____
_____
_____

(MY) GOAL FOR WHAT I'M WORKING ON AND CREATING:

_____
_____
_____

I AM:
My affirmation for today

ADDITIONAL NOTES, THOUGHTS, REFLECTIONS, VIBES AND GRATITUDE:

What are you doing to get closer to your goals, intentions, and wellness? What are the challenges you are facing? What else comes up during your day to reflect on?

MY DAILY VIBE

"Confidence is silence. Insecurities are loud."

Date: _____

❤️ (MY) WELL-BEING CHECK IN:
How I'm feeling

....
....
....

🙌 (MY) GRATITUDE TODAY:
What, who and things I'm grateful for

....
....
....

📅 (MY) INTENTION FOR TODAY:
What I hope/intend to accomplish or even create today?

....
....
....

🎯 (MY) GOAL FOR WHAT I'M WORKING ON AND CREATING:

....
....
....

💪 I AM:
My affirmation for today

ADDITIONAL NOTES, THOUGHTS, REFLECTIONS, VIBES AND GRATITUDE:

What are you doing to get closer to your goals, intentions, and wellness? What are the challenges you are facing? What else comes up during your day to reflect on?

MY DAILY VIBE

"Create! There will never be another today."
- IAN DAVIS

Date: _____

❤️ (MY) WELL-BEING CHECK IN:
How I'm feeling

....
....
....

🙌 (MY) GRATITUDE TODAY:
What, who and things I'm grateful for

....
....
....

📅 (MY) INTENTION FOR TODAY:
What I hope/intend to accomplish or even create today?

....
....
....

🎯 (MY) GOAL FOR WHAT I'M WORKING ON AND CREATING:

....
....
....

💪 I AM:
My affirmation for today

ADDITIONAL NOTES, THOUGHTS, REFLECTIONS, VIBES AND GRATITUDE:

What are you doing to get closer to your goals, intentions, and wellness? What are the challenges you are facing? What else comes up during your day to reflect on?

MY DAILY VIBE

*"Creative mind.
Creative Vibes.
Creative Life."*

Date: _____

♡ (MY) WELL-BEING CHECK IN:
How I'm feeling

....
....
....

🙌 (MY) GRATITUDE TODAY:
What, who and things I'm grateful for

....
....
....

📅 (MY) INTENTION FOR TODAY:
What I hope/intend to accomplish or even create today?

....
....
....

🎯 (MY) GOAL FOR WHAT I'M WORKING ON AND CREATING:

....
....
....

💪 I AM:
My affirmation for today

....

ADDITIONAL NOTES, THOUGHTS, REFLECTIONS, VIBES AND GRATITUDE:

What are you doing to get closer to your goals, intentions, and wellness? What are the challenges you are facing? What else comes up during your day to reflect on?

MY DAILY VIBE

"Creative possibilities are available to you. Each day brings new opportunities to lean toward fear or lean into love. May your day unfold with ease and grace. May you connect to the ever-present energy of love Within and around you."

- IAN DAVIS

Date: _____

(MY) WELL-BEING CHECK IN:
How I'm feeling

....
....
....

(MY) GRATITUDE TODAY:
What, who and things I'm grateful for

....
....
....

(MY) INTENTION FOR TODAY:
What I hope/intend to accomplish or even create today?

....
....
....

(MY) GOAL FOR WHAT I'M WORKING ON AND CREATING:

....
....
....

I AM:
My affirmation for today

ADDITIONAL NOTES, THOUGHTS, REFLECTIONS, VIBES AND GRATITUDE:

What are you doing to get closer to your goals, intentions, and wellness? What are the challenges you are facing? What else comes up during your day to reflect on?

MY DAILY VIBE

"Creatives hustle harder."
- IAN DAVIS

Date: _____

♡ (MY) WELL-BEING CHECK IN:
How I'm feeling

....
....
....

🙌 (MY) GRATITUDE TODAY:
What, who and things I'm grateful for

....
....
....

📅 (MY) INTENTION FOR TODAY:
What I hope/intend to accomplish or even create today?

....
....
....

🎯 (MY) GOAL FOR WHAT I'M WORKING ON AND CREATING:

....
....
....

💪 I AM:
My affirmation for today

ADDITIONAL NOTES, THOUGHTS, REFLECTIONS, VIBES AND GRATITUDE:

What are you doing to get closer to your goals, intentions, and wellness? What are the challenges you are facing? What else comes up during your day to reflect on?

MY DAILY VIBE

"Discipline is just choosing between what you want now and what you want most."

- DALE PARTRIDGE

Date: _____

(MY) WELL-BEING CHECK IN:
How I'm feeling

....
....
....

(MY) GRATITUDE TODAY:
What, who and things I'm grateful for

....
....
....

(MY) INTENTION FOR TODAY:
What I hope/intend to accomplish or even create today?

....
....
....

(MY) GOAL FOR WHAT I'M WORKING ON AND CREATING:

....
....
....

I AM:
My affirmation for today

ADDITIONAL NOTES, THOUGHTS, REFLECTIONS, VIBES AND GRATITUDE:

What are you doing to get closer to your goals, intentions, and wellness? What are the challenges you are facing? What else comes up during your day to reflect on?

MY DAILY VIBE

"Do it with passion or not at all."
- ROSA NOUCHETTE CAREY

Date: _____

(MY) WELL-BEING CHECK IN:
How I'm feeling

....
....
....

(MY) GRATITUDE TODAY:
What, who and things I'm grateful for

....
....
....

(MY) INTENTION FOR TODAY:
What I hope/intend to accomplish or even create today?

....
....
....

(MY) GOAL FOR WHAT I'M WORKING ON AND CREATING:

....
....
....

I AM:
My affirmation for today

ADDITIONAL NOTES, THOUGHTS, REFLECTIONS, VIBES AND GRATITUDE:

What are you doing to get closer to your goals, intentions, and wellness? What are the challenges you are facing? What else comes up during your day to reflect on?

MY DAILY VIBE

"Do not dwell in the past, do not dream of the future, concentrate the mind on the present moment."

- HEBREWS 10:35, NIV

Date: _____

(MY) WELL-BEING CHECK IN:
How I'm feeling

....
....
....

(MY) GRATITUDE TODAY:
What, who and things I'm grateful for

....
....
....

(MY) INTENTION FOR TODAY:
What I hope/intend to accomplish or even create today?

....
....
....

(MY) GOAL FOR WHAT I'M WORKING ON AND CREATING:

....
....
....

I AM:
My affirmation for today

ADDITIONAL NOTES, THOUGHTS, REFLECTIONS, VIBES AND GRATITUDE:

What are you doing to get closer to your goals, intentions, and wellness? What are the challenges you are facing? What else comes up during your day to reflect on?

MY DAILY VIBE

"Don't allow your thoughts to be on anything you don't want."

Date: _____

(MY) WELL-BEING CHECK IN:
How I'm feeling

....
....
....

(MY) GRATITUDE TODAY:
What, who and things I'm grateful for

....
....
....

(MY) INTENTION FOR TODAY:
What I hope/intend to accomplish or even create today?

....
....
....

(MY) GOAL FOR WHAT I'M WORKING ON AND CREATING:

....
....
....

I AM:
My affirmation for today

....

ADDITIONAL NOTES, THOUGHTS, REFLECTIONS, VIBES AND GRATITUDE:

What are you doing to get closer to your goals, intentions, and wellness? What are the challenges you are facing? What else comes up during your day to reflect on?

MY DAILY VIBE

"Don't chase people. Be an example. Attract them. Work hard and be yourself. The people who belong in your life will come find you and stay. Just do your thing."

Date: _____

(MY) WELL-BEING CHECK IN:
How I'm feeling

....
....
....

(MY) GRATITUDE TODAY:
What, who and things I'm grateful for

....
....
....

(MY) INTENTION FOR TODAY:
What I hope/intend to accomplish or even create today?

....
....
....

(MY) GOAL FOR WHAT I'M WORKING ON AND CREATING:

....
....
....

I AM:
My affirmation for today

ADDITIONAL NOTES, THOUGHTS, REFLECTIONS, VIBES AND GRATITUDE:

What are you doing to get closer to your goals, intentions, and wellness? What are the challenges you are facing? What else comes up during your day to reflect on?

BE SO GOOD THEY CAN'T IGNORE YOU

— STEVE MARTIN

MY TARGETS FOR THE MONTH OF: _____

NOTES

MY DAILY VIBE

"Don't cry over the past, it's gone. Don't stress about the future, it hasn't arrived. Live in the present and make it beautiful."

Date: _____

(MY) WELL-BEING CHECK IN:
How I'm feeling

....
....
....

(MY) GRATITUDE TODAY:
What, who and things I'm grateful for

....
....
....

(MY) INTENTION FOR TODAY:
What I hope/intend to accomplish or even create today?

....
....
....

(MY) GOAL FOR WHAT I'M WORKING ON AND CREATING:

....
....
....

I AM:
My affirmation for today

....

ADDITIONAL NOTES, THOUGHTS, REFLECTIONS, VIBES AND GRATITUDE:

What are you doing to get closer to your goals, intentions, and wellness? What are the challenges you are facing? What else comes up during your day to reflect on?

MY DAILY VIBE

"Don't downgrade your dream just to fit your reality. Upgrader your conviction to match your destiny."

- JOHN ASSARAF

Date: _____

(MY) WELL-BEING CHECK IN:
How I'm feeling

....
....
....

(MY) GRATITUDE TODAY:
What, who and things I'm grateful for

....
....
....

(MY) INTENTION FOR TODAY:
What I hope/intend to accomplish or even create today?

....
....
....

(MY) GOAL FOR WHAT I'M WORKING ON AND CREATING:

....
....
....

I AM:
My affirmation for today

ADDITIONAL NOTES, THOUGHTS, REFLECTIONS, VIBES AND GRATITUDE:

What are you doing to get closer to your goals, intentions, and wellness? What are the challenges you are facing? What else comes up during your day to reflect on?

MY DAILY VIBE

"Don't forget to be awesome."

Date: _____

(MY) WELL-BEING CHECK IN:
How I'm feeling

....
....
....

(MY) GRATITUDE TODAY:
What, who and things I'm grateful for

....
....
....

(MY) INTENTION FOR TODAY:
What I hope/intend to accomplish or even create today?

....
....
....

(MY) GOAL FOR WHAT I'M WORKING ON AND CREATING:

....
....
....

I AM:
My affirmation for today

ADDITIONAL NOTES, THOUGHTS, REFLECTIONS, VIBES AND GRATITUDE:

What are you doing to get closer to your goals, intentions, and wellness? What are the challenges you are facing? What else comes up during your day to reflect on?

MY DAILY VIBE

"Don't judge each day by the harvest you reap but by the seeds that you plant."

- ROBERT LOUIS STEVENSON

Date: _____

(MY) WELL-BEING CHECK IN:
How I'm feeling

....
....
....

(MY) GRATITUDE TODAY:
What, who and things I'm grateful for

....
....
....

(MY) INTENTION FOR TODAY:
What I hope/intend to accomplish or even create today?

....
....
....

(MY) GOAL FOR WHAT I'M WORKING ON AND CREATING:

....
....
....

I AM:
My affirmation for today
....

ADDITIONAL NOTES, THOUGHTS, REFLECTIONS, VIBES AND GRATITUDE:

What are you doing to get closer to your goals, intentions, and wellness? What are the challenges you are facing? What else comes up during your day to reflect on?

MY DAILY VIBE

"Don't make a habit of choosing what feels good over what is actually good for you."

- ERIC THOMAS

Date: _____

(MY) WELL-BEING CHECK IN:
How I'm feeling

....
....
....

(MY) GRATITUDE TODAY:
What, who and things I'm grateful for

....
....
....

(MY) INTENTION FOR TODAY:
What I hope/intend to accomplish or even create today?

....
....
....

(MY) GOAL FOR WHAT I'M WORKING ON AND CREATING:

....
....
....

I AM:
My affirmation for today

ADDITIONAL NOTES, THOUGHTS, REFLECTIONS, VIBES AND GRATITUDE:

What are you doing to get closer to your goals, intentions, and wellness? What are the challenges you are facing? What else comes up during your day to reflect on?

MY DAILY VIBE

"Don't quit"

Date: _____

(MY) WELL-BEING CHECK IN:
How I'm feeling

....
....
....

(MY) GRATITUDE TODAY:
What, who and things I'm grateful for

....
....
....

(MY) INTENTION FOR TODAY:
What I hope/intend to accomplish or even create today?

....
....
....

(MY) GOAL FOR WHAT I'M WORKING ON AND CREATING:

....
....
....

I AM:
My affirmation for today

....

ADDITIONAL NOTES, THOUGHTS, REFLECTIONS, VIBES AND GRATITUDE:

What are you doing to get closer to your goals, intentions, and wellness? What are the challenges you are facing? What else comes up during your day to reflect on?

MY DAILY VIBE

"Don't raise your voice. improve your argument."
- DESMOND TUTU

Date: _____

(MY) WELL-BEING CHECK IN:
How I'm feeling

....
....
....

(MY) GRATITUDE TODAY:
What, who and things I'm grateful for

....
....
....

(MY) INTENTION FOR TODAY:
What I hope/intend to accomplish or even create today?

....
....
....

(MY) GOAL FOR WHAT I'M WORKING ON AND CREATING:

....
....
....

I AM:
My affirmation for today

ADDITIONAL NOTES, THOUGHTS, REFLECTIONS, VIBES AND GRATITUDE:

What are you doing to get closer to your goals, intentions, and wellness? What are the challenges you are facing? What else comes up during your day to reflect on?

MY DAILY VIBE

"Don't talk fear, talk faith!"

Date: _____

(MY) WELL-BEING CHECK IN:
How I'm feeling

....
....
....

(MY) GRATITUDE TODAY:
What, who and things I'm grateful for

....
....
....

(MY) INTENTION FOR TODAY:
What I hope/intend to accomplish or even create today?

....
....
....

(MY) GOAL FOR WHAT I'M WORKING ON AND CREATING:

....
....
....

I AM:
My affirmation for today

ADDITIONAL NOTES, THOUGHTS, REFLECTIONS, VIBES AND GRATITUDE:

What are you doing to get closer to your goals, intentions, and wellness? What are the challenges you are facing? What else comes up during your day to reflect on?

MY DAILY VIBE

"Don't tell people your dreams. Show them."

Date: _____

❤️ (MY) WELL-BEING CHECK IN:
How I'm feeling

....
....
....

🙌 (MY) GRATITUDE TODAY:
What, who and things I'm grateful for

....
....
....

📅 (MY) INTENTION FOR TODAY:
What I hope/intend to accomplish or even create today?

....
....
....

🎯 (MY) GOAL FOR WHAT I'M WORKING ON AND CREATING:

....
....
....

💪 I AM:
My affirmation for today

ADDITIONAL NOTES, THOUGHTS, REFLECTIONS, VIBES AND GRATITUDE:

What are you doing to get closer to your goals, intentions, and wellness? What are the challenges you are facing? What else comes up during your day to reflect on?

MY DAILY VIBE

"Don't wait for it to happen, go make it happen."

Date: _____

(MY) WELL-BEING CHECK IN:
How I'm feeling

....
....
....

(MY) GRATITUDE TODAY:
What, who and things I'm grateful for

....
....
....

(MY) INTENTION FOR TODAY:
What I hope/intend to accomplish or even create today?

....
....
....

(MY) GOAL FOR WHAT I'M WORKING ON AND CREATING:

....
....
....

I AM:
My affirmation for today

ADDITIONAL NOTES, THOUGHTS, REFLECTIONS, VIBES AND GRATITUDE:

What are you doing to get closer to your goals, intentions, and wellness? What are the challenges you are facing? What else comes up during your day to reflect on?

MY DAILY VIBE

"Don't wait for the right opportunity. Create it."
- GEORGE BERNARD SHAW

Date: _____

(MY) WELL-BEING CHECK IN:
How I'm feeling

....
....
....

(MY) GRATITUDE TODAY:
What, who and things I'm grateful for

....
....
....

(MY) INTENTION FOR TODAY:
What I hope/intend to accomplish or even create today?

....
....
....

(MY) GOAL FOR WHAT I'M WORKING ON AND CREATING:

....
....
....

I AM:
My affirmation for today

ADDITIONAL NOTES, THOUGHTS, REFLECTIONS, VIBES AND GRATITUDE:

What are you doing to get closer to your goals, intentions, and wellness? What are the challenges you are facing? What else comes up during your day to reflect on?

MY DAILY VIBE

"Don't wait. The time will never be just right."
- NAPOLEON HILL

Date: _____

(MY) WELL-BEING CHECK IN:
How I'm feeling

....
....
....

(MY) GRATITUDE TODAY:
What, who and things I'm grateful for

....
....
....

(MY) INTENTION FOR TODAY:
What I hope/intend to accomplish or even create today?

....
....
....

(MY) GOAL FOR WHAT I'M WORKING ON AND CREATING:

....
....
....

I AM:
My affirmation for today

ADDITIONAL NOTES, THOUGHTS, REFLECTIONS, VIBES AND GRATITUDE:

What are you doing to get closer to your goals, intentions, and wellness? What are the challenges you are facing? What else comes up during your day to reflect on?

MY DAILY VIBE

"Don't wish for it work for it."

Date: _____

(MY) WELL-BEING CHECK IN:
How I'm feeling

....
....
....

(MY) GRATITUDE TODAY:
What, who and things I'm grateful for

....
....
....

(MY) INTENTION FOR TODAY:
What I hope/intend to accomplish or even create today?

....
....
....

(MY) GOAL FOR WHAT I'M WORKING ON AND CREATING:

....
....
....

I AM:
My affirmation for today

....

ADDITIONAL NOTES, THOUGHTS, REFLECTIONS, VIBES AND GRATITUDE:

What are you doing to get closer to your goals, intentions, and wellness? What are the challenges you are facing? What else comes up during your day to reflect on?

MY DAILY VIBE

"Don't worry about the future or worry, but know that worrying is as effective as trying to solve an algebra equation by chewing bubble gum."

- BAZ LUHRMANN

Date: _____

(MY) WELL-BEING CHECK IN:
How I'm feeling

....
....
....

(MY) GRATITUDE TODAY:
What, who and things I'm grateful for

....
....
....

(MY) INTENTION FOR TODAY:
What I hope/intend to accomplish or even create today?

....
....
....

(MY) GOAL FOR WHAT I'M WORKING ON AND CREATING:

....
....
....

I AM:
My affirmation for today

....

ADDITIONAL NOTES, THOUGHTS, REFLECTIONS, VIBES AND GRATITUDE:

What are you doing to get closer to your goals, intentions, and wellness? What are the challenges you are facing? What else comes up during your day to reflect on?

MY DAILY VIBE

"Dream big, work hard, stay focused and surround yourself with good people."

Date: _____

❤️ (MY) WELL-BEING CHECK IN:
How I'm feeling

....
....
....

🙌 (MY) GRATITUDE TODAY:
What, who and things I'm grateful for

....
....
....

📅 (MY) INTENTION FOR TODAY:
What I hope/intend to accomplish or even create today?

....
....
....

🎯 (MY) GOAL FOR WHAT I'M WORKING ON AND CREATING:

....
....
....

💪 I AM:
My affirmation for today

....

ADDITIONAL NOTES, THOUGHTS, REFLECTIONS, VIBES AND GRATITUDE:

What are you doing to get closer to your goals, intentions, and wellness? What are the challenges you are facing? What else comes up during your day to reflect on?

MY DAILY VIBE

"Dreams don't work unless you do."
- JOHN C. MAXWELL

Date: _____

(MY) WELL-BEING CHECK IN:
How I'm feeling

....
....
....

(MY) GRATITUDE TODAY:
What, who and things I'm grateful for

....
....
....

(MY) INTENTION FOR TODAY:
What I hope/intend to accomplish or even create today?

....
....
....

(MY) GOAL FOR WHAT I'M WORKING ON AND CREATING:

....
....
....

I AM:
My affirmation for today

....

ADDITIONAL NOTES, THOUGHTS, REFLECTIONS, VIBES AND GRATITUDE:

What are you doing to get closer to your goals, intentions, and wellness? What are the challenges you are facing? What else comes up during your day to reflect on?

MY DAILY VIBE

"Each day is a fresh start with a clean slate. The past is gone and the future isn't here yet – own the now. May you Give yourself permission to feel good,– To be aware, abundant, fulfilled and be your best."

— IAN DAVIS

Date: _____

(MY) WELL-BEING CHECK IN:
How I'm feeling

....
....
....

(MY) GRATITUDE TODAY:
What, who and things I'm grateful for

....
....
....

(MY) INTENTION FOR TODAY:
What I hope/intend to accomplish or even create today?

....
....
....

(MY) GOAL FOR WHAT I'M WORKING ON AND CREATING:

....
....
....

I AM:
My affirmation for today

....

ADDITIONAL NOTES, THOUGHTS, REFLECTIONS, VIBES AND GRATITUDE:

What are you doing to get closer to your goals, intentions, and wellness? What are the challenges you are facing? What else comes up during your day to reflect on?

MY DAILY VIBE

"Each day is a new birth unlimited with miraculous possibilities. May your thinking be clear with purpose. May your heart be free to love. May you free your mind from all limitation and lack. May you embody the energy of love."

- IAN DAVIS

Date: _____

(MY) WELL-BEING CHECK IN:
How I'm feeling

....
....
....

(MY) GRATITUDE TODAY:
What, who and things I'm grateful for

....
....
....

(MY) INTENTION FOR TODAY:
What I hope/intend to accomplish or even create today?

....
....
....

(MY) GOAL FOR WHAT I'M WORKING ON AND CREATING:

....
....
....

I AM:
My affirmation for today

ADDITIONAL NOTES, THOUGHTS, REFLECTIONS, VIBES AND GRATITUDE:

What are you doing to get closer to your goals, intentions, and wellness? What are the challenges you are facing? What else comes up during your day to reflect on?

MY DAILY VIBE

"Ego Says: "Once everything falls into place, I'll feel peace."
Spirits says: "Find your peace, and then everything will fall into place.""
- MARIANNE WILLIAMSON

Date: _____

(MY) WELL-BEING CHECK IN:
How I'm feeling

....
....
....

(MY) GRATITUDE TODAY:
What, who and things I'm grateful for

....
....
....

(MY) INTENTION FOR TODAY:
What I hope/intend to accomplish or even create today?

....
....
....

(MY) GOAL FOR WHAT I'M WORKING ON AND CREATING:

....
....
....

I AM:
My affirmation for today

ADDITIONAL NOTES, THOUGHTS, REFLECTIONS, VIBES AND GRATITUDE:

What are you doing to get closer to your goals, intentions, and wellness? What are the challenges you are facing? What else comes up during your day to reflect on?

MY DAILY VIBE

"Either I will find a way, or i will make one."
- PHILIP SIDNEY

Date: _____

(MY) WELL-BEING CHECK IN:
How I'm feeling

....
....
....

(MY) GRATITUDE TODAY:
What, who and things I'm grateful for

....
....
....

(MY) INTENTION FOR TODAY:
What I hope/intend to accomplish or even create today?

....
....
....

(MY) GOAL FOR WHAT I'M WORKING ON AND CREATING:

....
....
....

I AM:
My affirmation for today

ADDITIONAL NOTES, THOUGHTS, REFLECTIONS, VIBES AND GRATITUDE:

What are you doing to get closer to your goals, intentions, and wellness? What are the challenges you are facing? What else comes up during your day to reflect on?

MY DAILY VIBE

"Either you run the day, or the day runs you."
- JIM ROHN

Date: _____

❤️ (MY) WELL-BEING CHECK IN:
How I'm feeling

....
....
....

🙌 (MY) GRATITUDE TODAY:
What, who and things I'm grateful for

....
....
....

📅 (MY) INTENTION FOR TODAY:
What I hope/intend to accomplish or even create today?

....
....
....

🎯 (MY) GOAL FOR WHAT I'M WORKING ON AND CREATING:

....
....
....

💪 I AM:
My affirmation for today

ADDITIONAL NOTES, THOUGHTS, REFLECTIONS, VIBES AND GRATITUDE:

What are you doing to get closer to your goals, intentions, and wellness? What are the challenges you are facing? What else comes up during your day to reflect on?

MY DAILY VIBE

"Energy, like the bibilial grain of mustard see, will move mountains."
- HOSEA BALLOU

Date: _____

❤️ (MY) WELL-BEING CHECK IN:
How I'm feeling

....
....
....

🙌 (MY) GRATITUDE TODAY:
What, who and things I'm grateful for

....
....
....

📅 (MY) INTENTION FOR TODAY:
What I hope/intend to accomplish or even create today?

....
....
....

🎯 (MY) GOAL FOR WHAT I'M WORKING ON AND CREATING:

....
....
....

💪 I AM:
My affirmation for today

ADDITIONAL NOTES, THOUGHTS, REFLECTIONS, VIBES AND GRATITUDE:

What are you doing to get closer to your goals, intentions, and wellness? What are the challenges you are facing? What else comes up during your day to reflect on?

MY DAILY VIBE

"Every artist was once an amateur."
- RALPH WALDO EMERSON

Date: _____

❤️ (MY) WELL-BEING CHECK IN:
How I'm feeling

....
....
....

🙌 (MY) GRATITUDE TODAY:
What, who and things I'm grateful for

....
....
....

📅 (MY) INTENTION FOR TODAY:
What I hope/intend to accomplish or even create today?

....
....
....

🎯 (MY) GOAL FOR WHAT I'M WORKING ON AND CREATING:

....
....
....

💪 I AM:
My affirmation for today

ADDITIONAL NOTES, THOUGHTS, REFLECTIONS, VIBES AND GRATITUDE:

What are you doing to get closer to your goals, intentions, and wellness? What are the challenges you are facing? What else comes up during your day to reflect on?

MY DAILY VIBE

"Every word you speak and every thought you think is an affirmation for your future."

- CHERYL RICHARDSON

Date: _____

(MY) WELL-BEING CHECK IN:
How I'm feeling

....
....
....

(MY) GRATITUDE TODAY:
What, who and things I'm grateful for

....
....
....

(MY) INTENTION FOR TODAY:
What I hope/intend to accomplish or even create today?

....
....
....

(MY) GOAL FOR WHAT I'M WORKING ON AND CREATING:

....
....
....

I AM:
My affirmation for today

ADDITIONAL NOTES, THOUGHTS, REFLECTIONS, VIBES AND GRATITUDE:

What are you doing to get closer to your goals, intentions, and wellness? What are the challenges you are facing? What else comes up during your day to reflect on?

MY DAILY VIBE

"Everyone you meet is fighting a battle you know nothing about. be kind. Always."

- BRAD MELTZER

Date: _____

(MY) WELL-BEING CHECK IN:
How I'm feeling

....
....
....

(MY) GRATITUDE TODAY:
What, who and things I'm grateful for

....
....
....

(MY) INTENTION FOR TODAY:
What I hope/intend to accomplish or even create today?

....
....
....

(MY) GOAL FOR WHAT I'M WORKING ON AND CREATING:

....
....
....

I AM:
My affirmation for today

ADDITIONAL NOTES, THOUGHTS, REFLECTIONS, VIBES AND GRATITUDE:

What are you doing to get closer to your goals, intentions, and wellness? What are the challenges you are facing? What else comes up during your day to reflect on?

MY DAILY VIBE

"Everything in the universe is within you. Ask all from yourself."
- RUMI

Date: _____

(MY) WELL-BEING CHECK IN:
How I'm feeling

....
....
....

(MY) GRATITUDE TODAY:
What, who and things I'm grateful for

....
....
....

(MY) INTENTION FOR TODAY:
What I hope/intend to accomplish or even create today?

....
....
....

(MY) GOAL FOR WHAT I'M WORKING ON AND CREATING:

....
....
....

I AM:
My affirmation for today

....

ADDITIONAL NOTES, THOUGHTS, REFLECTIONS, VIBES AND GRATITUDE:

What are you doing to get closer to your goals, intentions, and wellness? What are the challenges you are facing? What else comes up during your day to reflect on?

MY DAILY VIBE

"Excellence is my presence, never tense, never hesitant."
- NOTORIOUS BIG

Date: _____

(MY) WELL-BEING CHECK IN:
How I'm feeling

....
....
....

(MY) GRATITUDE TODAY:
What, who and things I'm grateful for

....
....
....

(MY) INTENTION FOR TODAY:
What I hope/intend to accomplish or even create today?

....
....
....

(MY) GOAL FOR WHAT I'M WORKING ON AND CREATING:

....
....
....

I AM:
My affirmation for today

ADDITIONAL NOTES, THOUGHTS, REFLECTIONS, VIBES AND GRATITUDE:

What are you doing to get closer to your goals, intentions, and wellness? What are the challenges you are facing? What else comes up during your day to reflect on?

MY DAILY VIBE

"Excellence is never an accident; it is the result of high intention, sincere effort, intelligent direction, skillful execution and the vision to see obstacles as opportunities."

— ANONYMOUS

Date: _____

(MY) WELL-BEING CHECK IN:
How I'm feeling

....
....
....

(MY) GRATITUDE TODAY:
What, who and things I'm grateful for

....
....
....

(MY) INTENTION FOR TODAY:
What I hope/intend to accomplish or even create today?

....
....
....

(MY) GOAL FOR WHAT I'M WORKING ON AND CREATING:

....
....
....

I AM:
My affirmation for today

ADDITIONAL NOTES, THOUGHTS, REFLECTIONS, VIBES AND GRATITUDE:

What are you doing to get closer to your goals, intentions, and wellness? What are the challenges you are facing? What else comes up during your day to reflect on?

MY DAILY VIBE

"Faith is taking the first step even when you don't see the whole staircase."
- DR. MARTIN LUTHER KING JR.

Date: _____

(MY) WELL-BEING CHECK IN:
How I'm feeling

_____
_____
_____

(MY) GRATITUDE TODAY:
What, who and things I'm grateful for

_____
_____
_____

(MY) INTENTION FOR TODAY:
What I hope/intend to accomplish or even create today?

_____
_____
_____

(MY) GOAL FOR WHAT I'M WORKING ON AND CREATING:

_____
_____
_____

I AM:
My affirmation for today

ADDITIONAL NOTES, THOUGHTS, REFLECTIONS, VIBES AND GRATITUDE:

What are you doing to get closer to your goals, intentions, and wellness? What are the challenges you are facing? What else comes up during your day to reflect on?

MY DAILY VIBE

"Figure out your weakness and don't make it your weakness anymore."
-STACEY LEWIS

Date: _____

(MY) WELL-BEING CHECK IN:
How I'm feeling

....
....
....

(MY) GRATITUDE TODAY:
What, who and things I'm grateful for

....
....
....

(MY) INTENTION FOR TODAY:
What I hope/intend to accomplish or even create today?

....
....
....

(MY) GOAL FOR WHAT I'M WORKING ON AND CREATING:

....
....
....

I AM:
My affirmation for today

ADDITIONAL NOTES, THOUGHTS, REFLECTIONS, VIBES AND GRATITUDE:

What are you doing to get closer to your goals, intentions, and wellness? What are the challenges you are facing? What else comes up during your day to reflect on?

RISK vs REWARD IS THE NEW ROI.

- REBEKAH GRIPPA

MY TARGETS FOR THE MONTH OF: _____

NOTES